GRANDMOTHERS
STORIES

For Bjorn and Jonas — B. M.

To the memory of Joyce and Phyllis, my children's grandmothers,
and for my sister Rhiannon — S. B.

Barefoot Books
124 Walcot Street
Bath BA1 5BG

First published in Great Britain in 1999 by Barefoot Books, Ltd
This paperback edition first published in 2006. All rights reserved. No part of this book may be
reproduced in any form or by any means, electronic or mechanical, including photocopying, recording
or by any information storage and retrieval system, without permission in writing from publisher

This book has been printed on 100% acid-free paper

Graphic design by Jennie Hoare, Bradford on Avon
Colour separation by Grafiscan, Verona
Printed and bound in Singapore by Tien Wah Press Pte Ltd

This book was typeset in Bembo 14pt
The illustrations were prepared in gouache on Hollingsworth cartridge

Paperback ISBN 1-84686-010-5

British Cataloguing-in-Publication Data:
a catalogue record for this book is available from the British Library

3 5 7 9 8 6 4

GRANDMOTHERS' STORIES

WISE WOMAN TALES
FROM MANY CULTURES

retold by
BURLEIGH MUTÉN

illustrated by
SIÂN BAILEY

Barefoot Books
Celebrating Art and Story

Contents

$\mathcal{J}$NTRODUCTION

THE WISE WOMAN was once as well known and reliable as the ground we stand upon. She held the knowledge of what went before. She was the keeper of tradition, the storyteller, the teacher, healer and leader of her people. In many traditions, grandmother's wisdom was considered the voice of Earth herself.

When societies shifted away from matriarchy, the roles of women were redefined and the wise woman was banished to an invisible place, thereafter appearing in our folktales as foolish or wicked. Despite the stories of nasty old witches and silly old women that filled my childhood, I had two grandmothers whose loving kindness and wisdom poured into my heart. At a very early age an old woman began to appear in my dreaming, always there to turn me away from danger.

It is my great pleasure to provide you with images of the wise woman as a benevolent, resourceful, independent, informed guide, who is respected in her community. She is determined and bold and trusts her own capable mind to figure out how to rescue herself in 'The Old Woman who was Not Afraid'. She is the benevolent witch — she who gifts her community — in 'The Beautiful Crone of Córdoba'. She is the calm protectress who even knows how to handle the spirit world in 'Go Ask the Wise Woman'. As 'Old Mother Holle', she teaches the importance of helping others, rewarding hard work and kindness. She is the village midwife, known to all in her community in 'The Midwife and the Djinn'. And lastly, in 'The Old Woman who was Right', she knows how to make others value and appreciate her. May these wise women remind us who our grandmothers are and of the many qualities they possess.

Burleigh Mutén
Amherst, Massachusetts, 1999

'GRANDMOTHER, will you tell us a story?' said the children.

'Of course I will tell you a story,' Grandmother said. 'Which one shall I tell you today?'

'Tell the one about the old woman who flies on the crow,' said the girl.

'No, tell the one about the old woman who is not afraid,' said the boy.

'You are my Grandma,' said the little boy. 'I want the one about the old woman and the babies.'

Grandmother laughed. She lifted the little boy on to her lap.

'I will tell you all of those stories,' she said. 'And if you are very quiet, I will tell you some stories you have not heard before.'

The girl and the boy stretched out on the rug next to Grandmother's rocking chair. And the little one stayed on her lap.

THE *M*IDWIFE AND THE DJINN

SENEGALESE

ONCE THERE WAS A LITTLE OLD WOMAN named Old Fatu who helped every woman in her village when their babies were born. Old Fatu rubbed the mothers' backs. She carried special bark for them to chew. She sang encouraging words. And when the babies were born, Old Fatu swaddled them in soft cloth and laid them in their mothers' arms. Everyone in the village knew Old Fatu because she was the first person who had held them when they were new.

One night, while Old Fatu was sleeping in her house on the edge of the village, there was a knock on her door. She was not surprised. Many children are born after the sun goes down. She yawned as she shuffled across her house in the dark. 'How many babies have I helped into this world?' she said to herself. 'It must be nine hundred — and here comes one more.'

She opened her door, and she let out a <u>hoot!</u> There, on her doorstep, stood a shimmering djinn who was so tall that he had to bend over to greet her. Before Old Fatu could think, the djinn reached out his long arm and grabbed her hand. Before she could resist, he pulled her right out into the dark street.

Old Fatu was frightened. She had no idea why a djinn should come to her house. She had no idea why he was pulling her through the streets of the village, but she knew there was no sense in saying a word. She knew that djinns don't talk to people, and she knew that there was no escaping a djinn, so she just ran alongside that big fellow as fast as she could. They ran past the market next to the sea.

They ran all the way to the edge of the village and then they were running on streets that Old Fatu had never seen before.

Old Fatu was out of breath. Her legs were strong, but they began to creak. She stumbled and fell down. The djinn saw how hard it was for the old woman to run so quickly beside him. He helped her to stand up. Then he eased his grip on her hand and he slowed down a little. Now Old Fatu could tell that the djinn would bring her no harm.

The djinn pulled Old Fatu through a narrow alley and up two flights of stone stairs, and then suddenly they were standing before a magnificent palace made of pink stone. Old Fatu had lived all her life in this village but she had never seen a palace like this. She looked up and down the street. She did not know how they could still be in her village. She followed the djinn through long, tiled hallways with ceilings that reached high above the big djinn's head. She followed him through courtyards full of big, leafy plants and pools full of goldfish. She followed him up a long curving staircase, which climbed over a fountain, and finally she followed that djinn into a room where a beautiful woman djinn was lying in bed. Old Fatu immediately noticed the beads which the woman was wearing. They looked like big nuggets of honey around her neck.

The djinn woman was not much bigger than Old Fatu, but her belly was as round as the moon. Old Fatu took one look at the djinn woman and she understood why the djinn had brought her here. Their baby had been trying to be born for a long time. The djinn woman was tired. Her hair was damp from working so hard, and she wanted someone to help her.

Old Fatu held the djinn woman's hand. She carefully put her ear next to the big round belly and listened. 'I know what you need,' she thought to herself. Then Old Fatu reached into the pouch that hung on a cord around her waist. She pulled out a piece of soft bark and she showed it to the djinn woman. Old Fatu broke off a small piece, held it up to her mouth and pretended to chew. Then she handed the bark to the woman. The djinn woman studied the peculiar soft bark. Old Fatu nodded and smiled, and she continued to pretend

to chew. The djinn woman smiled and nodded, and she put the soft bark into her mouth.

Old Fatu did what she always did with mothers. She rubbed the djinn woman's shoulders. She placed a cool cloth on the woman's forehead and she began to sing. When the child came out of its mother's body, the room filled with golden streams of light. Old Fatu did what she always did with new babies. She looked at the baby's miniature body and saw that it was a perfect little djinn boy. She laid him on a soft cloth, whispered a prayer for his long life, and lifted the tiny boy into his mother's arms.

The djinn woman was so full of joy that she laughed out loud. The djinn man hugged her and kissed the top of her head. They stroked their baby's little feet and touched his tiny fingers. The djinn woman smiled at Old Fatu. She nodded as if to say thank you.

Suddenly, the djinn woman looked surprised. She quickly handed the baby to the djinn, and she put both of her hands on to her belly, which was starting to tremble. She looked straight at Old Fatu as if to say, 'What is happening now?'

Old Fatu carefully placed her ear on the woman's big belly and listened. She smiled at the djinn woman and held up two fingers. 'Two babies are coming tonight!' she said. Again she gave the djinn woman a piece of bark to chew. She rubbed the djinn woman's shoulders and she placed a cool cloth on her forehead. Then Old Fatu began to sing.

A few minutes later the child was born, and again the room filled with streams of golden light. Old Fatu looked at the child's miniature body and saw that it was a perfect little djinn girl. She laid her on a soft cloth, whispered a prayer for her long life, and lifted the tiny girl into her mother's arms. The djinn hugged his woman and they both laughed out loud. They were so happy to have a girl and a boy.

Old Fatu sighed and sat down at the foot of the bed. 'Djinn twins!' thought Old Fatu. 'Now that's something you don't see every day.' Just then the djinn mother began to look surprised again. She quickly handed the girl baby to the djinn, and she put both hands on to her belly, which had started to tremble again. Old Fatu hurried to put her ear on the djinn woman's belly and she listened. This time she held up three fingers. 'Three babies are coming tonight!' she said.

She gave the woman another piece of bark, and again she rubbed the djinn woman's shoulders. She placed a cool cloth on her forehead.

And then she began to sing.

A few minutes later the baby was born and the room filled with streams of golden light again. Everyone laughed with pleasure. Old Fatu looked at the baby's small body and she saw that this one was another perfect little djinn boy. 'Djinn triplets!' thought Old Fatu. 'Now that is something you don't see every day.' She laid the baby on a soft cloth, whispered a prayer for his long life, and she began to place the tiny boy in his mother's arms. But just as the djinn mother reached out to take the child from Old Fatu, she cried out in surprise again. 'Another baby!' thought Old Fatu. 'This djinn is popping out babies like seeds flying out of a pod!' Old Fatu quickly handed the third baby to the djinn and she listened to the djinn woman's belly. This time Old Fatu held up four fingers. 'Four babies are coming tonight!' she cried. Before she could rub the djinn woman's shoulders or bring her a cold cloth, the baby began to be born. Old Fatu looked at the baby's miniature body, and she saw that it was another perfect little djinn girl. She laid the baby on a soft cloth, said a prayer for her long life, and lifted the tiny girl into her mother's arms.

'Two girls and two boys,' said Old Fatu to herself. 'Djinn quadruplets! Now that is a rare treat.' But that was not all! Right after the second girl, a third baby boy was born, and right after that a third baby girl was born. 'Djinn sextuplets!' cried Old Fatu. 'Now this is a night to remember!'

Old Fatu sat down in a chair. She was tired and she was hoping to take a nap. She looked at the new djinn family and smiled. 'Bless you all,' she said. 'And thank you for asking Old Fatu to help. There is nothing as special as new-born babies. Many, many blessings to you, for you have sextuplets: three girls and three boys!'

Then the djinn woman and her children and the tall djinn man began to fade so that Old Fatu could see right through them. She blinked. 'Are these old eyes playing tricks on me?' she wondered. Old Fatu closed her eyes for a moment and rubbed them. When she opened them a few seconds later, the woman and the babies and the tall djinn man had disappeared. The bed was empty, and then the bed and the room and the palace faded and disappeared completely. Old Fatu felt as if she was zooming through a tunnel of beautiful, coloured lights. Then suddenly she found herself standing beneath a tree in the market next to the sea. It was still night. There was no one around but the moon gleaming on the quiet water.

14

15

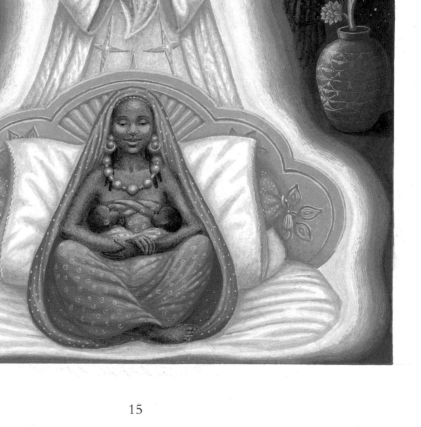

'Have I been flying in my sleep?' she asked herself. 'How did I get way down here by the shore? Were those djinns a dream?' she wondered as she began to walk home. 'I am so old that I don't know when I am dreaming and when I'm awake,' she said to herself.

When Old Fatu got back to her little house it was nearly morning. The stars had disappeared and the sky was turning light blue and pale pink. Old Fatu was tired and she was hungry. She yawned and leaned against her front door. 'Dear me,' she said to herself, 'I'd better go straight to bed. I don't know how I got to town. I don't know where that djinn palace could be in this village, and I don't even know if I'm awake or dreaming. I'm a weary old woman, that's what I am.'

Old Fatu pushed open the door. She gasped and she put her hand up to her mouth, for there, on her table, was a bowl full of ripe juicy mangoes and a cauldron of hot peanut soup. Old Fatu fell into her chair, astonished. She feasted until she was full, and then she fell into a deep sleep right there in her chair. She was so tired that she slept for two days and two nights. When she awoke the cauldron of soup and the bowl full of mangoes were still on her table. 'Then it wasn't a dream,' she said to herself.

Old Fatu walked out to the stream behind her house. She scooped some water into her pitcher, and she heard an odd jingling sound. 'What am I hearing?' she said. 'It's these old ears that are playing tricks on me now!' She poured the water into a basin, and again she heard the jingling sound. She reached into the bowl and pulled out handfuls of gold coins. 'Those djinns!' she said to herself. 'They are really too kind.'

That afternoon, Old Fatu bought a fish at the market for her dinner. When she got home, she cut open the fish to clean it. 'What's this?' she cried. 'More gifts?' Inside the fish were the djinn woman's necklace and a pair of honey-nugget earrings. 'Wherever you are, thank you,' she called out. 'Whoever you are, may your children live one hundred years.' Then she thought for a moment, and she called out again, 'You are djinns — may your children live for a million years!'

Old Fatu washed the amber necklace and the earrings. They glistened in the sunlight and looked like giant beads of honey.

Old Fatu slid the necklace over her head. She felt the beads with her hand. Then she put on the earrings. Old Fatu thought of the djinn woman surrounded by all her babies and she smiled.

Old Fatu lived a life of ease after the night when she had helped the djinn woman give birth to her children. She had so much gold that she never had any worries. She held feasts for the children of the village every Sunday, and she never stopped helping the women of her village when they gave birth to their babies. Through the years many people admired Old Fatu's amber jewellery. Some people even offered to buy the necklace from her. 'Oh no,' Old Fatu would reply. 'Someone very, very special gave it to me.' Then she would laugh as she remembered the night the djinn woman gave birth to six golden babies.

THE OLD WOMAN WHO WAS NOT AFRAID

JAPANESE

ONCE THERE WAS a poor old woman who didn't have much in the world, just a small garden and an even smaller house. Every day she pounded rice into flour for dumplings. She steamed the dumplings, and she sold them for a little money. Everyone loved the old woman's dumplings as they were the sweetest in town.

One day, she dropped a whole plate of dumplings. And those little round dumplings rolled right out of the door. They rolled down the path and over the road. They rolled into the woods and kept right on rolling until they bumped into a tree where they stopped.

The old woman chased her dumplings into the woods. Just as she bent down to pick up her dumplings, someone reached out and grabbed them and ran off deeper into the woods.

'Hey!' yelled the old woman. 'That's my supper!'

She knew that an Oni had stolen her dumplings. Everyone in Japan knows that Onis are hairy little creatures with horns who live in the woods. They are always hungry and love to eat sweets. Most people leave them alone, but the old woman was so angry, she ran after the Oni who had stolen her supper. She chased the Oni into a hole in the side of a hill that led into a tunnel that went down inside the earth. Suddenly she found herself standing in a large, wide cave full of Onis. The Onis were wildly chewing her dumplings, smiling and laughing and licking their lips with glee.

'Who is the cook who made these scrumptious sweet dumplings?' the Oni leader asked.

The old woman liked to be praised for her dumplings, and for a moment she forgot that the Onis had eaten her supper. 'I am the cook who made those dumplings,' she proudly said.

The Oni leader bowed to the old woman and the rest of the Onis cheered. When she looked at all those Onis licking their lips, the old woman suddenly remembered that they had just eaten her supper. 'Yes, I am the one who picked the rice,' she said. 'I am the one who pounded the rice and patted the flour into round little dumplings. And I am the one who cooked the dumplings for my supper, not yours! And I am still hungry, you rude little thieves!'

'Oh dear,' said the Oni leader, and the rest of the Onis grew quiet. 'Old Woman, your dumplings were so scrumptious, we quite forgot our manners. Now will you please be our guest? Will you cook your supper right here in our kitchen?' he asked. 'You can make plenty of dumplings, and we will all have dumplings for supper!'

The Onis shouted and cheered for more dumplings. Their voices were loud in the large, wide cave and they rubbed their bellies. 'More dumplings! More dumplings!' they yelled.

The old woman followed the Oni leader to the Oni kitchen. 'Goodness me!' she said to herself. 'I am alone in this cave with a whole pack of Onis. How will I ever get out of here?' But she was not afraid. 'I'll think of something,' she said to herself. 'I'll find a way to get out of this Oni cave.'

An underground stream ran through the Oni kitchen. The Oni leader dipped a bucket into the stream, filling a large pot with water. He put the pot over the fire, then handed the old woman one grain of rice. 'Put this rice in the water,' he said.

'You must be joking,' said the old woman. 'One grain of rice will not make a meal for a family of mice. If you want dumplings for your whole family, I will need much more rice than this.'

The Oni laughed and picked up a long red spoon with a dragon carved into its handle. He stirred the pot with the long red spoon and the single grain of rice turned into ten. 'Now you try it,' he said.

The old woman stirred the rice with the long red spoon. The ten grains of rice turned into twenty. She stirred the rice again. The twenty grains of rice turned into thirty. Soon the pot was full. 'Well, isn't this the perfect spoon!' said the old woman.

She made supper for everyone. And while she quietly ate her dumplings, the Onis were laughing and talking and stuffing their dumplings into their mouths as if they had not eaten in weeks. Then as soon as they finished, they shouted for more. Their voices were loud in the large, wide cave, but the old woman was not afraid.

'Don't they ever stop eating?' she said to herself. 'I'll be cooking all day. I'll be cooking all night as long as I'm trapped in this Oni cave. But I'll think of something, I'll find a way to get out of this Oni cave.'

She returned to the Oni kitchen. This time she filled the pot with water herself. She put one grain of rice into the pot and stirred it with the long red spoon. Just as before, the single grain of rice turned into ten. She stirred the rice again. The ten grains of rice turned into twenty. And soon the pot was full.

She pounded the rice into flour, patted the flour into dumplings and steamed them. Then she served another big batch of dumplings to the Onis. Just as before, they gobbled them up and cheered for more. This time, when the old woman went to the stream to fill the pot with water, she remembered that Onis do not know how to swim. Not only that, Onis do not even travel in boats.

'If I had a boat,' she thought, 'I could float down this stream. If I could float down this stream, I could find a way to get out of this Oni cave.' Then she thought of the big rice pot and made a plan.

Now the old woman sang while she put the rice into the pot. And she sang while she stirred the rice with the long red spoon. She sang while she pounded the rice into flour. And she sang while she patted the flour into dumplings.

The Onis liked the old woman's singing. Her soft voice made them feel sleepy. And by the time the dumplings were ready to eat, the Onis were sound asleep.

The old woman dragged the big rice pot down to the stream and climbed into it, pushing it out into the stream with the long red spoon. But she was so excited, she forgot to sing and the Onis woke up. When they saw the old woman floating down the stream in the rice pot, they began to yell. The whole pack of Onis came running to the stream. 'More dumplings! More dumplings!' they shouted.

Now there was only one way the Onis could stop the old woman. They bent down on their knees and began to drink up the water in the stream. They slurped and they slurped until their cheeks were bulging with water.

The more the Onis slurped up the stream, the smaller the stream became. Soon there was barely any water in the stream, and the old

woman's boat slowed down. But she was not afraid. 'I will think of something,' she said to herself. 'I will get out of this Oni cave.'

Now there was so little water in the stream that fish started jumping into the old woman's boat. She grabbed hold of the fish, and she threw them at the Onis. 'Fill your bellies with fish!' she shouted. And she kept right on paddling with the long red spoon.

The hungry little Onis opened their mouths to catch the fish. The stream water gushed out of their mouths and filled up the stream, and the old woman's boat sailed quickly away. 'Goodbye, Onis,' she shouted. 'Goodbye, goodbye, goodbye!'

Soon she could not see the Onis at all. She sailed along through the rushing stream in the big rice pot. And after a while, the stream flowed through a hole in the cave out into the light of day. The old woman climbed out of the pot, took the long red spoon and ran through the woods to the road and up the path. She ran into her house and slammed the door. Then she started to sing and went straight to work. She filled up her rice pot with water, dropped one grain of rice into the pot and stirred it with the long red spoon. Sure enough, the single grain of rice turned into ten. She stirred again and, sure enough, the ten grains turned into twenty. Soon the pot was full.

With the help of the long red spoon, the old woman made enough dumplings each day to feed the whole town. So she opened a restaurant on the porch of her house and people came from far away to eat her dumplings. The old woman made a lot of money by selling her scrumptious sweet dumplings, and soon she was one of the richest women in all of Japan. Even so, every night after she had closed the restaurant, she walked down to the tree where she had first seen the Oni and left a big plate of dumplings for all the hungry little Onis.

GRANDMOTHER'S BASKET

RUSSIAN

ONCE LONG AGO, there was a man whose wife gave birth to twins. The girl was named Tanya and the boy was named Vanya. When Tanya and Vanya were very young, their mother died. The man could not take care of the children all by himself, so he married a woman to take care of Tanya and Vanya.

I'm sorry to say that the new stepmother did not like children. After their father had gone to work in the morning, she yelled at Tanya and Vanya. She sent them outside, and she would not let them back into the house until dusk.

'You no-good snippets,' said Stepmother, 'get into the bath and wash your sooty little snippet selves. Put on your pyjamas and get into bed before your father comes home.'

Stepmother did not kiss the twins goodnight. She did not tell

27

them a story. 'No talking in bed!' she hissed from the other side of the door.

One morning after the twins' father had gone to work, Stepmother said to herself, 'I've got an idea. I'll get rid of those no-good little snippets once and for all.'

She called to the children: 'Tanya, Vanya, my sweethearts. I want you two darlings to visit my granny. She lives in the hut in the heart of the woods. She's old and she needs you to help her. My granny loves children. You'll see.'

Stepmother hugged and kissed Tanya and Vanya. 'Goodbye, my sweeties,' she said.

So Tanya and Vanya walked towards the woods. They stopped at the top of the hill, looking down at their father's house. There was Stepmother, watching and waving goodbye. She was even smiling.

'She's never been this nice before,' Tanya said to Vanya. 'Let's ask our grandmother what she thinks about this. Let's pay a visit to Grandmother before we go to the old granny's hut in the heart of the woods.'

Tanya and Vanya walked until they could no longer see Stepmother. They walked until they were sure she could no longer see them. Then they ran straight to their grandmother's house.

Grandmother was gathering wood. She saw the twins coming and hurried to meet them. She opened her arms and hugged them close to her. 'Grandmother, something is wrong,' said Tanya. 'Stepmother kissed us.'

'Grandmother, something is wrong,' said Vanya. 'Stepmother hugged us. She called us her sweeties.'

'What could be wrong about that?' said Grandmother.

'She's never kissed us before,' said Tanya. 'She's never hugged us before.'

'She's never called us her sweeties,' said Vanya. 'And she's sending us to help her old granny who lives in the hut in the heart of the woods.'

'Bow sha moy!' exclaimed Grandmother. 'Your stepmother is not sending you to her granny. The old woman who lives in the hut in the heart of the woods is a woodwitch. Stepmother is sending you to the woodwitch who likes to eat children!'

'Oh no!' cried Tanya.

'What shall we do?' said Vanya.

Grandmother gave Tanya and Vanya a basket. She put a jar of milk, a chunk of meat and some bread into the basket. Then she bent down on her knees and looked straight into Tanya and Vanya's eyes. 'Now you know who the woodwitch is and you will not be fooled,' she said. 'Remember to be polite to everyone you meet. Be kind to everyone you meet. And look for the right moment to escape.'

Grandmother squeezed the children's hands and gave them her blessing. 'While we're apart, you will be in my heart,' she said.

Tanya and Vanya walked slowly back to the woods. They barely spoke a word to each other. They walked until they came to the wood-witch's hut.

'I'm afraid to knock on the door,' said Vanya.

'Remember what Grandmother said,' whispered Tanya. 'We know who the woodwitch is. We will not be fooled. We will be polite and kind to everyone we meet.'

'And we will look for the right moment to escape,' said Vanya.

Tanya knocked on the door.

'Who's there?' growled the wood-witch.

'It's Tanya and Vanya,' said the twins. 'Stepmother sent us to help you, Granny. What can we do to help?'

The old woodwitch opened the door. She was as thin as a broomstick and as pale as the moon. She looked at the twins and licked her lips.

'Come right in, my sweeties,' she croaked. 'Girl, use your tasty little fingers to weave me a shawl.' And she handed Tanya a box of yarn.

She turned to Vanya: 'Boy, use your tasty little fingers to carry some water. Fill the barrel at the back of the hut with this bucket.' And she handed him a bucket full of holes.

Tanya and Vanya looked at each other and did not say a word.

The woodwitch put on her big clunking boots and picked up her prickly staff. 'If you don't finish this work by the time I get back,' she hissed, 'I'll eat you for supper.' And off she stomped, slamming the door behind her.

Vanya went out to find the barrel behind the hut. Poor Tanya sat staring at the loom. She didn't know the first thing about weaving and her eyes filled with tears. Just then, hundreds of mice scurried up the sides of the loom. 'We are the mice who live in the walls,' said one of them.

Tanya remembered what Grandmother had said. She bowed to the mice. 'Pleased to meet you,' she said politely.

'We know how to weave,' said the mouse. 'We will make a shawl for the witch.'

'You are so kind!' said Tanya. Then she noticed that the mice were thin. 'Wouldn't you like some bread?' she asked.

She reached into Grandmother's basket, pulled out the bread and broke it into tiny crumbs. The mice ate the bread and set to work weaving a shawl for the woodwitch.

When the shawl was finished, Tanya thanked them. 'You saved my life,' she said.

Outside she found Vanya, dipping the bucket into the well. The water was pouring through the holes in the bucket as fast as he could fill it.

'Oh dear,' said Tanya.

'Oh dear is right,' said Vanya.

The woodwitch's cat sat watching the twins. 'I am the cat who lives with the witch,' it said.

Tanya and Vanya remembered what Grandmother had said and they bowed politely to the cat. 'Pleased to meet you,' they said.

'Put some leaves in the bucket,' said the cat. 'And cover the leaves with mud to patch the holes.'

'You are so kind!' said Tanya. Then she noticed that the cat was thin. 'Wouldn't you like some milk?' she asked.

She reached into Grandmother's basket, took out the jar of milk and poured it into a saucer. The cat lapped up the milk and licked its whiskers. Vanya patched the bucket and filled the barrel with water. When the barrel was full, the twins thanked the cat. 'You saved my life,' said Vanya.

Just then, the woodwitch stomped into the house. 'So you wove me a shawl!' she grumbled. She stomped out to the barrel. 'So you filled the barrel!' she growled. 'Tomorrow your tasks will be harder.'

In the morning she told Tanya to weave two shawls and told

Vanya to cut down a tree and split it into logs. She put on her big clunking boots and picked up her prickly staff. 'If you don't finish this work before I get back,' she hissed, 'I will eat you for supper.' And off she stomped, slamming the door behind her.

The twins watched her through the window. They watched until the woodwitch was gone. 'This is the right moment to escape,' said Vanya.

'Let's go!' said Tanya.

The twins opened the door but the woodwitch's dog began to snarl. The twins remembered what Grandmother had said. 'Pleased to meet you,' they said. And they bowed politely.

Vanya noticed the dog looked thin. 'Wouldn't you like some meat?' he asked. He reached into Grandmother's basket, pulled out the chunk of meat and fed it to the dog.

'You are kind,' said the dog. 'I can help you with two things. When you hear the wind swooshing behind you, throw down this piece of glass. When you hear the old grump huffing and puffing behind you, throw down this comb.'

The twins quickly thanked the dog. Tanya put the glass in her pocket, Vanya put the comb in his and they ran for their lives.

When the woodwitch returned to the hut, the children were gone. The cat was licking the last drops of milk from the saucer. 'You no-good cat!' said the witch. 'Why didn't you stop those no-good snippets? They were my supper.'

'What about my supper?' asked the cat. 'What about my supper for the last ten years? You feed yourself but you never feed me. The twins gave me milk!' And the cat licked its lips.

The woodwitch ran outside. Her watchdog was snoring. 'You no-good dog!' said the witch. 'Why didn't you stop those no-good snippets? They were my supper.'

'What about my supper?' said the dog. 'What about my supper for the last ten years? You feed yourself but you never feed me. The twins gave me meat!' And the dog licked its lips.

'For tooten snooten!' cried the woodwitch. And she kicked the wall with her big clunking boots three times. Then she grabbed her broom from the corner and took off after the twins.

Tanya and Vanya were running as fast as they could. They were

running for their lives. They heard the wind swooshing behind them. It was the sound of the witch's broom.

'Throw down the glass!' yelled Vanya. Tanya threw the glass down on the ground behind her, and a wide lake stretched out between the witch and the twins. The woodwitch screeched to a halt because witches cannot cross over water.

'Those nasty no-good snippets!' she cried.

The twins ran for their lives. The witch flew around the shore of the lake and soon the twins heard her huffing and puffing behind them. The woodwitch was right behind them now.

'Throw down the comb!' yelled Tanya. Vanya threw the comb down on the ground behind them and a huge wall of thick trees grew up between the witch and the twins.

The woodwitch crashed into the trees, her broom broke in two and she fell to the ground. She kicked and pounded. And she tried to squeeze through the wall of trees. But no matter what she did, the woodwitch could not get through.

Tanya and Vanya ran all the way to Grandmother's house. She saw them coming and ran out to meet them. She opened her arms and hugged the twins close to her for a very long time.

'Oh, Grandmother,' cried the twins, 'we're so glad to see you!'

'Tanya and Vanya,' said Grandmother, 'I'm so glad to see you!'

The twins told their father what had happened. They told him that Stepmother had sent them to help the woodwitch. They told him about the mice and the cat and the dog. And they told him about Grandmother's basket. Their father sent Stepmother away. He told her not to come back.

'I will be glad to take care of Tanya and Vanya while you are at work,' said Grandmother.

'Good idea,' said their father.

'Great idea!' said the twins.

THE *W*OMAN IN THE MOON

HAWAIIAN

OLD HEENA was the oldest woman in the village. No one knew exactly how old Old Heena was, but she knew all the stories and songs from the beginning of time. She had raised twenty-two children of her own. She had tended her gardens and fished and cooked for her family. Now she was old. She was tired and she wanted to rest.

Heena napped after breakfast. She napped after lunch and supper too. One day, while Heena was tilling her garden, she leaned her weary old head on the end of her hoe. And she was so tired that she fell asleep standing up!

That was the day Heena had an important dream. In her dream, she was resting in a large, wide hammock, rocking back and forth. In her dream, her husband and children were working in her garden

while she rested in the large, wide hammock. 'Ah,' said Heena when she woke up. 'Wouldn't it be lovely to rest all the time?'

But her children's children still needed teaching and the garden still needed tending. Dinner still needed to be cooked every night. So Heena kept right on working even though she was tired and wanted to rest more than anything else.

One day, when her husband came home from his boat, he found Heena napping on the porch with one of her grandchildren asleep in her lap. He clapped his hands and startled Old Heena awake. 'You lazy old woman!' he cried. 'Sleeping all day while there's work to be done.' He took the child off Old Heena's lap and pulled Heena out of the chair. 'Look at that garden of yours! Full of weeds! Full of

beetles! You lazy old woman, tend to your garden and make my supper. And when you've done that, my boat needs to be cleaned.'

Old Heena sighed deeply. 'I wish I could find a place where I could rest all the time,' she said to herself.

Rainbow heard Heena's wish and, knowing how hard Heena had worked all her life, arched down into Heena's garden. Old Heena stepped back in wonder at Rainbow's bright glowing colours. Then she saw a path in Rainbow's blue band that led up into the sky. 'Glory me!' she said. 'What is this spectacular sight?'

'This is your wish, old girl,' replied Rainbow. 'You have worked hard all your life, and you have been kind to others. Now take the blue path to the rest you have earned.'

Heena looked over her shoulder at her husband. She looked down at the beetles and weeds. Then she stepped on to Rainbow's blue path and looked up at the sun. 'I'll take my rest in the sun's lap,' she said to herself. 'Sun is bright and warm.'

The higher Old Heena got, the hotter it got. She peeked her head through the clouds. Sun's light was so bright, she had to close her eyes. Sun's heat was so strong, it curled her hair and pinched her face and arms. 'Ouch!' she cried. 'I can take a hint, Sun. I'll leave you alone.' Old Heena was glad to slide down the path away from the sun's heat. She slid all the way down the blue path until she was back on Earth in her garden. It was night now. Heena saw her husband carrying a bucket of water from the well. He was grumbling about his lazy wife who had gone off without bringing water into the house.

40

43

To this day the people of Hawaii look up to the night sky to see the Woman in the Moon. They don't call her Heena any more, for that was her earthly name. Now she is called Lono Moku, which means 'Lame Lono', because of her broken foot. Look up in the sky when the moon is full, and you will see Lono Moku, the Woman in the Moon, who worked hard all her life and was kind to others. Look up in the night sky at the Woman in the Moon who is still taking a good, long rest.

THE *B*EAUTIFUL CRONE OF CÓRDOBA

MEXICAN

L ONG AGO, before you were born, there was a beautiful old crone whose magic was known far and wide. La Bruha could make the corn grow high for the farmers when there was no rain. She could tell the miners where to find silver and gold in the mountains. And she knew where the fish could be caught in the sea.

Nearly everyone in the city of Córdoba went to La Bruha for help at least once in their lives. She smiled as she gazed into her crystal ball. She smiled as she cast a magic spell. Everyone knew that La Bruha was a witch, but she was so kind and so helpful, no one seemed to mind.

Her hair was as white as the snow on the mountains. Her eyes were as blue as the sea and her skin as soft as velvet. Although she was old, La Bruha walked through the city with quick, strong strides.

She was as beautiful as a young girl. Some people said La Bruha was friends with the devil because of her unusual ways. But most agreed this was a ridiculous notion.

One night, as La Bruha was mixing a magic potion for a lovesick boy, someone banged loudly at her door. As always, she opened it gladly. Ten policemen and their captain rushed into her house. They surrounded La Bruha and tied her hands with a rope. As they pushed her out into the street, she called over her shoulder to the boy, 'Don't worry about me. Drink the potion with your sweetheart and you will be married within a year.'

La Bruha then turned to the policemen and smiled her enchanting smile. She was so beautiful, they couldn't help smiling back. The Captain bowed to La Bruha and held out his arm to help her into his wagon. Then he took her to the Judge's chamber.

The Judge looked up from behind his tall desk. 'So you have caught the old witch,' he said.

La Bruha looked straight into the Judge's eyes and smiled her enchanting smile. She was so beautiful, the Judge couldn't help smiling at her. Her long white hair made him think of a glorious waterfall. So he closed his eyes. He shook his head. He banged his gavel and said, 'No witch will live in this city, no matter how beautiful she is.'

La Bruha kept right on looking straight into the Judge's eyes. Her gaze made him think of the stars. Before he knew what he was doing, he smiled again. Then he shook his head. He banged his gavel and said, 'No witch will live in this city, no matter how lovely she is!'

La Bruha smiled her enchanting smile. And she kept right on looking straight into the Judge's eyes. The Judge stood up. He pounded his gavel three times on his desk. 'No beautiful witch will put me under her spell, no matter how much I wish she would! Lock up this crone in the third cellar of the jail before I change my mind!'

So the Captain and all ten policemen led La Bruha down the cold stone stairs into the first cellar. They led her down the cold stone stairs into the second cellar. At last they were all standing at the bottom of the cold stone stairs into the dark, damp hall of the third cellar. La Bruha smiled to herself when she saw her cell. There was a small, round stove and a narrow bed and nothing else.

'We are sorry, La Bruha,' said the Captain. 'You have helped us all with your magic. We do not want to leave you in this cold, dark place. But we must follow the Judge's orders.'

He bent down and lit a fire in the stove. Then he sent one of the policemen to bring La Bruha warm blankets. And he sent another to fetch her a soft velvet chair with wide arms and a footstool.

La Bruha smiled. 'Don't worry about me,' she said. 'For your kindness, I will tell you your fortunes. You will all be rich, your children will be famous and each of you will live to be a very old man.' She waved goodbye to them and settled down in the soft velvet chair.

47

Many days later, the Judge came to La Bruha's cell. He was sure that after she had lived in the third cellar all this time, she would confess to being a witch. He took the key from his belt, unlocked the door and cautiously entered her cell.

He was glad to see that La Bruha was facing the wall. He was afraid to look into her beautiful sparkling eyes again. Then he saw what La Bruha was doing. She was drawing with charcoal on the wall of her cell. She had drawn an enormous crow with widespread wings. On the back of the crow was an elaborate wicker basket big enough for a person to sit in. Every crisp black feather of the crow gleamed as if it were real.

'Come in, come in, Judge,' said La Bruha. 'Please sit down in this comfortable chair.'

The Judge nearly fell into the soft velvet chair, he was so surprised by the sight of the enormous crow that looked so real. 'You are an artist, La Bruha,' he said. 'This crow looks as if it is about to fly away.'

'You are too kind, Judge,' replied La Bruha. 'Will you please tell me this? In your view, is there anything missing from my drawing? Is there anything that this crow still needs?'

The Judge looked closely at the drawing. After a few moments, he said, 'The crow is perfect in every way, La Bruha. The only thing it could possibly need is someone to sit in the basket on the bird's back.'

'Good eye, Judge. Good eye,' said La Bruha. And she started to laugh. She laughed as she held her hand up to her drawing.

49

What happened next is so astounding, you may not believe it. The beautiful crone of Córdoba climbed into the basket on the crow's back. A strong wind blew through the room and the crow began to soar slowly across the wall. La Bruha looked straight into the Judge's eyes and smiled her enchanting smile. She lifted her hand and waved. The crow flew straight into the corner of the cell and disappeared!

The Judge rubbed his eyes. He shook his head and slapped his cheeks. He jumped out of the soft velvet chair and put his hands on the wall. The crow was gone. And so was the beautiful crone of Córdoba.

GO ASK THE WISE WOMAN

IRISH

L ONG, LONG AGO there was an old widow woman who lived on a farm with her daughter. Every day they milked their cows, fed their chickens and gathered the eggs. Every day they worked in their fields from dawn to dusk. Their cows gave rich milk. Their chickens laid large eggs. Their fields were full of rye and barley. The widow and her daughter were proud of their work.

Once, on the longest day of the summer, the widow and her daughter cut the rye in the largest field on their farm. It was hot that day, and they worked especially hard to cut and tie all the rye before the sun went down. When their work was done, the old widow and her daughter walked back to the house.

'Tonight I am too tired to make a proper meal,' said the old widow.

'Me, too,' said her daughter. 'You sit down, Mother, while I cut up some apples and cheese.'

'You are kind, Daughter,' said the widow. 'I am so tired, my feet are screaming!'

The daughter brought her mother a stool for her feet and made a meagre meal for them both.

'Tonight I am even too tired to take a proper bath,' said the widow.

'Me, too,' said her daughter.

So she filled a round, wooden tub with warm, soapy water. The two women pulled their chairs close to the tub and put their tired feet into the soothing water.

'Ahh,' said the widow. 'That feels fine.'

'Ahh,' said the daughter. 'Indeed it does.'

After a while the water in the tub grew cold. The widow and her daughter pushed their chairs back from the tub and dried their feet. They were so tired, they forgot to pour the feetwater out of the wooden tub. They were so tired, they dropped into their beds like two rocks falling into a puddle and they fell fast asleep.

Now, in those olden times, everyone knew about feetwater spirits. The widow and her daughter certainly knew about feetwater spirits, but they were so sound asleep, they did not hear the knock on the door. And they did not hear the voice that called to the water: 'Feetwater, Feetwater, open the door! Feetwater, Feetwater, let us in!'

The old widow and her daughter were so sound asleep, they didn't even hear the tub tumble over and break with a crash. Nor did they hear the feetwater spilling over the kitchen floor. But they did wake up when the door to the house was flung open. In rushed ten tiny women, each carrying a spinning wheel, and ten tiny men, each carrying a big bag of wool.

The tiny men pulled great wads of wool out of the bags and the tiny women wildly spun it into yarn. They were singing and laughing so loudly you would think they owned the old widow's house. This wildness went on for hours while the widow and her daughter lay in their beds, scared stiff.

'Whatever are we going to do?' the daughter whispered to her mother.

'Go ask the Wise Woman,' the mother whispered back.

'Of course,' said the daughter. She hopped out of bed, pretended she wasn't afraid and marched right into the kitchen. She grabbed hold of a bucket and called out, 'I'll be getting you hard workers some water for tea.' And she walked right through the kitchen and out of the door. The tiny men and the tiny women just kept right on with their work and their singing and laughing.

The old widow's daughter ran through the dark into the forest. She ran all the way to the Wise Woman's house. The Wise Woman was sitting on her porch with her cat in her lap. She was looking up at the stars.

The girl gasped and spluttered, 'Little men, women, wool, water, whoosh, laughing, yelling, feetwater.'

'Now, now,' the Wise Woman said. 'You are spluttering so, I cannot tell what you're saying.'

She put her arm around the old widow's daughter and took her inside for a cup of warm tea to calm her down.

55

The girl told the Wise Woman about the feetwater that she forgot to pour out. She told her about the ten tiny men and the ten tiny women who were wildly spinning in her mother's kitchen. The Wise Woman nodded when she heard the whole story. 'They are feetwater spirits, all right,' she said. 'They are up to no good. And their mischief will be bigger before it gets smaller, I can tell you that.'

The Wise Woman told the girl just what to do. So the girl ran back through the forest all the way to her mother's house. She peeked through the kitchen window. And sure enough, the small spirit people were still wildly working. They were still singing and laughing and making a terrible noise.

The widow's daughter followed the Wise Woman's advice. She flung open the kitchen door with a bang and shouted, 'Tee-cahdi in see-cahdi on the mountain! And it's all on fire! Bondia!'

Just as the Wise Woman had said, the small spirit people grabbed their belongings and they rushed out into the night. As soon as they were gone, the widow's daughter mopped up the last puddle of feet-water. She took the broken tub out to the shed and placed it upside down. She fetched a big rock from the garden and put it on top of the tub. Then she ran like the wind back into the house and bolted the door behind her.

'The spirits are gone!' the old widow said. 'You tricked the spirits out of the house. You are a brave girl, Daughter.'

'Wait!' said the daughter. 'We must close the windows and the curtains.'

So they ran through the house, closing every window and curtain. And they climbed back into their beds and waited. The house was so still that you could hear a pin drop.

Then, just as the Wise Woman had said, the feetwater spirits came back. They knocked on the door and shouted, 'Feetwater, Feetwater, open the door! Feetwater, Feetwater, let us in!'

But there was no answer.

The spirits knocked harder and shouted louder, 'Feetwater, Feetwater, open the door! Feetwater, Feetwater, let us in!'

Again there was no answer.

'Feetwater! Feetwater! Feetwater!!' the ten tiny men and the ten tiny women shouted together. 'Let us in!'

Finally the feetwater spoke: 'I can't let you in. I am down in the dirt under your tiny little stinking feet!'

The spirit men and women looked down at their little feet. They looked down at the dirt. They were so mad, they stomped up and down. Without feetwater, they were thwarted. Without feetwater, there was no way they could get into the old widow's house.

The widow and her daughter looked at each other and didn't say a word. After a while, the ten tiny men and the ten tiny women went away.

The old widow woman smiled at her daughter. 'Thanks to you,' she said, 'we are safe now.'

'Thanks to the Wise Woman,' the daughter said. And they went back to sleep.

After that night, no matter how tired the widow and her daughter were, they never forgot to pour out their feetwater. No matter how tired they were, they always poured their feetwater into the ground. Always.

OLD MOTHER HOLLE

GERMAN

ONCE THERE WAS a woman who had two daughters. One girl was her own flesh and blood and the other was her stepchild. This woman could not help loving her own dear daughter more than her stepdaughter. But that was no excuse for making her step-daughter do all the cooking and cleaning, and all the washing and spinning.

One day the stepdaughter cut her hand while she was spinning. Her spindle was stained with blood, so she took it down to the well to wash it. Her hand was weak from the cut and she dropped the spindle into the well.

She couldn't go home without her spindle. Her stepmother would be furious. So she climbed up on to the well and jumped in after it. Down she fell through the deep, dark water. And when she

rose to the surface, she found herself in the middle of a lake. On the edge of the lake she saw a little old woman working in her garden. The old woman's long white hair stretched out from her head like a snow storm when the wind makes the snow fly sideways. The girl swam to the shore, squeezed the water from her skirt and walked into the old woman's garden.

'Excuse me, old woman,' the girl said, 'I am Birchy.'

The old woman's great yellow horse teeth gleamed in the sunlight. She was really no taller than Birchy. In fact she was so small, Birchy found herself asking, 'May I help you?'

'Yes indeed, you may help me,' the old woman replied. 'I was just about to shake down these apples. Will you do this for me?'

'Of course I will,' said Birchy. And she wondered how the little old woman would have managed to climb the apple tree herself.

Birchy wiggled out on to the tree's strongest limb. As she rocked back and forth, the ripe apples dropped to the ground.

'Aren't you speedy!' the old woman said. 'I am Mother Holle, and I'm pleased to meet you, Birchy. Will you carry these apples into the house?'

'Of course I will,' said Birchy. And she wondered how the little old woman would have managed to carry the heavy basket by herself.

Old Mother Holle's house was full of the sweet smell of cinnamon bread baking in the oven. Birchy opened the door of the oven and peeked in. 'I'm ready to come out,' called the bread. 'Please be so kind as to lift me on to the table.'

'Bread can't talk,' Birchy said to herself. But she could see that the bread was right. Its crust was golden brown. Birchy put the bread on the table and the bread sang, 'Many thanks, many thanks!'

When the old woman saw the bread on the table, she smiled. And her great yellow horse teeth gleamed. 'Sit down by the fire, Birchy,' she said. 'I'll make some supper. How ever did you come to be swimming in my lake, dear?'

Birchy told Mother Holle about her stepmother and stepsister. She told her how she had cut her hand and dropped her spindle into the well. Mother Holle listened to every word. 'Aren't you a brave one!' she said when Birchy told her about jumping into the well.

That night the North Wind blew over the lake. The lake turned into ice. The wind whistled through the trees and the house began to tremble.

'This wind will be biting the old woman's bones,' Birchy thought to herself and she tiptoed to the old woman's bedside. Sure enough, Mother Holle's gleaming great horse teeth were chattering and clacking. And her bony old body was shaking with cold. Birchy unfolded the quilt at the bottom of the old woman's bed and shook it to fluff up its feathers. A puff of feathers blew out of a hole in the quilt, and it started to snow outside. Mother Holle stopped shivering, her teeth stopped clacking and she slept like a baby.

The next day, Mother Holle asked Birchy to shovel a path through the snow to the shore of the lake. 'Of course I will,' said Birchy.

The snow was heavy, Birchy's back ached and her
feet were cold, but she did not complain. She shovelled a
path through the snow all the way down to the lake.

That night the North Wind blew over the lake for a second time.
The lake turned into ice. The wind whistled through the trees and
the house began to tremble. Once again, Birchy tiptoed to the old
woman's bedside. She unfolded the quilt at the bottom of the old
woman's bed and shook it to fluff up its feathers. Again, a puff of
feathers flew out of the hole in the quilt. And again, it started to
snow outside. Mother Holle stopped shivering and slept like a baby.

63

In the morning Mother Holle asked Birchy to shovel a path around the lake. The snow was heavy, Birchy's back ached and her feet were cold, but she did not complain. She shovelled a path all the way around the lake.

That night the North Wind blew over the lake for a third time. The lake turned into ice. The wind whistled through the trees and the house began to tremble. Just as before, Birchy tiptoed to the old woman's bedside and unfolded the quilt to fluff up its feathers. Just then, the door of the house flew open and the North Wind rushed in and pulled a blizzard of feathers out of the hole in the quilt. Downy white feathers were swirling and twirling all over the house.

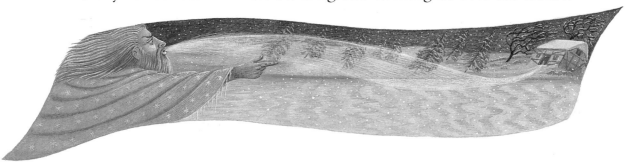

Just as before, when the feathers began to fly, it started to snow outside. And Old Mother Holle stopped shivering and slept like a baby. Birchy pushed against the North Wind with all her might. At last, she managed to slam the door shut. The feathers in Old Mother Holle's house were everywhere. There were feathers in the cauldron. There were feathers on the mantle. There were even feathers in the old woman's ears!

Birchy took the sheets from her own bed and quickly sewed them

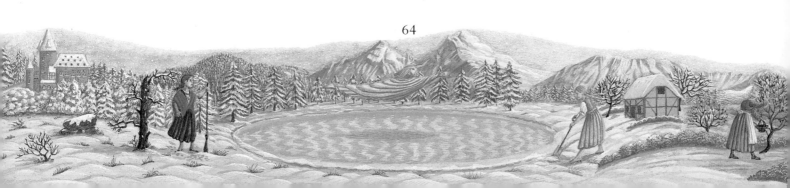

together. Then she stuffed all the feathers into the sheets and sewed the sheets shut. Birchy yawned. She snuggled under the soft feather quilt she had made. And she dreamed she was sleeping in her own little bed in her stepmother's house. In the morning Mother Holle was surprised to see Birchy sleeping beneath a puffy down quilt. 'Isn't she a clever girl!' Mother Holle said to herself.

Birchy opened her eyes. She was not in her own little bed at all. Old Mother Holle was standing right over her, smiling with her gleaming great horse teeth.

'You're such a smart girl!' said Mother Holle. 'You've made your-self a warm, downy quilt.'

Birchy smiled, but she felt sad inside. Old Mother Holle was kind, but Birchy missed her own little bed. She missed her stepsister and she even missed her stepmother. 'Mother Holle,' she said, 'I want to go home. When can I go home?'

'Right now, if you wish,' said Mother Holle. 'I will show you the way myself.'

She took Birchy's hand and they walked on the path Birchy had shovelled to the lake. They walked on the path Birchy had shovelled all around the lake. And they walked into the woods. The sun began to shine, and the snow began to melt. After a time they came to a waterfall rushing over the side of a hill. Mother Holle led Birchy into the waterfall. She squeezed Birchy's hand as the water poured over their heads. Birchy laughed. Old Mother Holle laughed. Then Mother Holle was gone. Birchy jumped out of the waterfall. She was no longer in the woods near Mother Holle's house. She was back at the well near her stepmother's house.

'Home!' she said to herself and started to skip through the woods. Just then, a huge, big-bellied bullfrog next to the well croaked, 'Shiny girl, shiny girl.'

'What ever does that frog mean?' Birchy said to herself. Then she saw that her dress had turned to gold. And in the pocket of her golden dress was her spindle, the one she had dropped into the well.

Now when Birchy's stepmother saw the golden dress, she wanted one for her own dear daughter.

'Thorny, you must jump into the well,' said the mother. 'Let me prick your finger so you can stain your spindle.'

So the woman pricked her own daughter's finger and stained the spindle with her dear daughter's blood. She threw the spindle into the well and then she pushed her in after it.

Now when Thorny found herself in the middle of the lake, she splashed and screamed, 'Help, Mother Holle, help!'

Mother Holle stood up in her garden. 'Dear me, what a loud one,' she said to herself. 'Don't you know how to swim, girl?' she called.

'Yes, I know how to swim,' Thorny shouted back.

'Then swim, girl. Swim now, and hush up!' Mother Holle said. 'Swim right to my shore.'

But Thorny was making so much noise, she couldn't hear Mother Holle. So Old Mother Holle climbed into her boat and rowed out to Thorny.

'I'm freezing,' Thorny moaned as the old woman helped her into the boat. 'I hope you have a fire going in that tiny little hut. I hate being wet.'

'Indeed I do,' said Mother Holle. And she thought to herself, 'This one's a doozy!'

So Thorny went straight into the house and Mother Holle went back to her work in the garden. Thorny smelled the sweet scent of cinnamon bread baking in the oven. She opened the oven door and peeked in. 'I'm ready to come out,' called the bread. 'Please be so kind as to lift me on to the table.'

'Bread can't talk,' said Thorny. 'Don't be ridiculous!' And she shut the oven door and sat down by the fire.

When her clothes were dry, she went outside to find Mother Holle. 'Can I help you, old woman?' she asked.

'Yes, you may help me,' Mother Holle replied. 'I was just about to shake down these rosy ripe apples. Will you do this for me?'

'Old women can't climb trees. Don't be ridiculous,' said Thorny. 'Watch me, Mother Holle.'

Thorny wiggled out on to the tree's lowest branch. But the branch was not strong and it broke. Thorny crashed into Mother Holle and they both fell down.

'Never mind,' said Mother Holle. 'Let's go inside. It's time for supper.'

'Hooray!' cried Thorny. 'I'm starving. What's for supper?'

'Warm bread fresh from the oven,' replied Mother Holle. But the bread had burned in the oven. So Mother Holle gave Thorny dry corn cakes and tea.

'How ever did you come to be swimming in my lake, dear?' asked Old Mother Holle.

Thorny lied to Mother Holle. She said she had cut her finger and fallen into the well. She pretended she didn't know about the waterfall or about the golden dress.

That night the North Wind blew over the lake. The lake turned into ice. The wind whistled through the trees and the house began to tremble.

'This cold is biting my bones,' Thorny said to herself. She could hear Mother Holle's gleaming great horse teeth chattering and clacking. She pulled her stepsister's puffy down quilt up over her ears and went back to sleep. It did not snow that night.

In the morning, Mother Holle asked Thorny to rake leaves. She took Mother Holle's rake and raked for a few minutes. Then she went back into the house. 'There's a blister on my thumb,' she grumbled. 'I can't do this kind of work. I'll ruin my soft smooth hands. What do I look like? Your slave?' And she stamped her foot.

Mother Holle had had enough. 'Never mind, girl,' she said. 'Would you like to see my waterfall?'

'Oh yes!' replied Thorny. And she said to herself, 'I'll get the dress and then I'll go home.'

Mother Holle took Thorny's hand. They walked around the lake, and they walked into the woods. After a time they came to the waterfall. Thorny let go of Mother Holle's hand and ran into the waterfall. 'Now I will be golden, too,' she said to herself. When she was sopping wet, she stepped out of the waterfall. And sure enough, she was next to the well near her mother's house. She looked down at her dress. It was covered with mud and wet weeds.

The huge, big-bellied bullfrog next to the well croaked, 'Slimy girl, slimy girl.'

Thorny cried all the way home. 'I don't know what I did wrong,' she sobbed.

'It's my fault,' said the mother when she heard the full story. 'I never taught you how to be kind. I never taught you how to work hard. And I never taught you to enjoy helping others. Well, I suppose it's about time you learned.'

Birchy helped Thorny take off her muddy dress. And she smiled.

THE OLD WOMAN WHO WAS RIGHT

SWEDISH

LONG, LONG AGO, there was an old woman whose husband had been cranking and complaining since the day they were married. Now that their children were grown and had homes of their own, the old woman was sick and tired of her husband's unkind words and his fault-finding ways.

One morning at breakfast, the old man banged his fist on the table, pushed his chair back and stood up. 'This porridge is too dry,' he snarled. 'You didn't cook the oats long enough, old woman. Can't you ever get it right?'

The old woman looked out of the window at the fields of wheat glowing gold in the morning sun. Then she banged her fist on the table, pushed her chair back and stood up. 'Yesterday, the porridge was too soft for you, old man. The day before, it was too thick.'

She walked around the table and stood next to her husband. She slipped her arm through his. 'For years you've been cranking about the way I cook. For years you've been cranking about the way I keep house. Now, listen to me, old man. Today I will go into the wheat fields to do your work. And you will stay here in the house to do mine.'

'You're too small to cut the wheat,' the old man grumbled. 'You couldn't do my work. You are too weak.'

'I am strong enough to do your work,' said the old woman. 'Are you clever enough to do mine?'

Well now, the old man could not let his wife insult him in this way. So he agreed to his wife's suggestion. He agreed to do her day of work in the house while she went into the fields to do his. The old woman put on her bonnet and smiled to herself.

'You'll be back before lunch, old woman,' said her husband. 'You'll soon see you're not fit for a day of hard work in the fields!'

'I'll be back for supper,' she called over her shoulder.

The old man poured himself a cup of coffee and sat down, thinking he would wait until his wife returned. He was sure she would be back within the hour. Meanwhile the old woman found the tools she would need to cut and gather the wheat. She put them into the wagon along with a bucket, six apples and three carrots from the garden. Then she hitched up the horse and headed for the fields.

While the old man sat at the table sipping his second and third cups of coffee, he began to wonder what had happened to his wife.

72

It was mid-morning and she still had not returned from the fields.

'Maybe she'll last until noon when the sun is high and hot,' he said to himself. 'Meanwhile I'll take care of some of her chores.'

He washed the dishes and made the beds. 'Working in the house is the life of ease,' he said to himself. 'I'll just take a nap for a few minutes here, as I'm sure she does every morning.' And he lay down and went to sleep.

While he was sleeping, the pig wandered into the house looking for its breakfast, which the old woman usually took to him at dawn. The old man woke up to a crash as the pig knocked over the compost bowl. The cow was groaning to be milked and the goat's bell was clanging as it threw its head back and forth between two fence posts where it was stuck.

The old man jumped out of bed, tripped over the pig and fell down the cellar steps, landing on his head which bulged with a big bump. He crawled over to the chest of ice and broke off a chunk to soothe the pain. 'A mug of cold ale is just what I need for this pain in my head,' he said to himself.

While he was filling his mug with ale, the old man heard the pig in the bedroom. Up he jumped and ran upstairs to catch it. Somehow he managed to capture the frisky creature and put it outside, cranking and complaining the whole time. Then he freed the goat from the fence. And as he milked the cow, cranking and complaining the whole time, she lifted her leg and gave him a swift hard kick on the other side of his head, which bulged up with another big bump.

'I'll go down to the cellar to get some ice and some ale to soothe this pain in my head,' he said to himself. But when he got to the bottom of the stairs, he saw that the cellar was flooded with ale. He had forgotten to close the tap when he had chased after the pig.

No sooner had the old man cleaned up the mess in the cellar than there was a knock at the door. One of his daughters had come to drop off her baby, as was her custom every day on her way into town. The child was sleeping when its mother left. And when the young thing woke up, it screamed until its face turned bright red.

The old man handed the baby a bottle of cow's milk. Then he remembered that he should have taken the cow out to pasture hours before. Not wanting to leave the baby, who was now quietly drinking its bottle of milk, the old man put the cow out to pasture on the sloping roof of the house where a fine bed of sweet grass had recently sprouted. He slipped a rope around the cow's neck, led it up on to the roof and dropped the free end of the rope down the chimney.

74

Then he ran like the wind back into the house and fastened the rope
to his own ankle so he would know if the cow began to wander
away. He put a pot of stew on the stove for supper, sat down at the
table and leaned back in his chair.

Up on the roof the cow was contentedly chomping the sweet
grass. She backed up to turn around, and fell off the roof, where she
dangled in mid-air from the rope.

Inside the house the rope jerked the old man out of his chair and
dragged him across the room into the chimney where he dangled
upside down. He let out a yell and the baby started to cry. The stew
on the stove boiled over the edge of the pot. The pot boiled dry and
the house began to fill with smoke. Just then, the old woman came
over the hill from the fields.

75

'What on earth is this?' she cried when she saw the cow dangling in mid-air. She ran up on to the roof of the house and cut the rope, holding it to let the cow slide down to the ground. She had no way of knowing but, by cutting the rope, she sent her husband crashing down the chimney into the fireplace, where of course he landed on his head.

'Where on earth is my husband?' she cried when she opened the door of her house and saw the room full of smoke.

'Here,' he croaked from the fireplace.

'Where?' she cried again, unable to see because of the smoke.

'Here,' he repeated. 'Here in the fireplace!'

Naturally when she heard this, the old woman thought her husband was on fire. So she grabbed the bucket of water she kept by the sink and threw it in the direction of the fireplace. Then, scooping up the yelling baby, she hunted in the smoke for the old man's arm and dragged him outside.

When they were a safe distance away from the house, the old woman noticed the rope tied around her husband's ankle. Now she understood what had happened when she had cut the cow's rope. She noticed the bumps on her husband's head. And she knew he had had a hard day in the house.

'Old woman, how was your day in the fields?' he asked. 'What work did you do?'

'I cut the west meadow all morning,' she said. 'When the sun was hot and high, I took the horse to the stream and we went for a

swim. Then I filled the bucket with water so the horse could have a long cool drink in the fields. I shared the apples and carrots with the horse for lunch. And then I tied the wheat into bundles and loaded them on to the wagon.'

She pointed to the wagon stacked higher than the house with bundles of wheat. 'Here is my day's work,' she said proudly.

Her husband pointed to the bumps on his head and he nodded towards the cow and the house, from which smoke was still pouring. 'Here is my day's work,' he said laughing. 'You were right, old woman. You were right to change places with me. Now I know how hard you work in the house. If you will go back to work in the house, I will go back to work in the fields. There will be no more cranking and complaining from this old man.'

'Very well,' she replied. 'Let's tend to those bumps on your head.'

They kissed and went back into the house. And, after that day, the old man had nothing but praise for his hard-working wife.

GRANDMOTHER smiled to herself.
The boy and the girl had fallen asleep
on the rug at her feet. But the little
boy was wide awake.

'Will you tell them again,
Grandma?' he asked. 'Will you tell
the old woman stories again?'

'Tomorrow,' Grandmother promised.
'I will tell them again tomorrow. But now it is
time for bed.'

SOURCES

THE CHARACTERS IN THESE STORIES sometimes use exclamations that have no meaning that I know of. These are: 'Tee-cahdi in see-cahdi' and 'Bondia!' ('Go Ask the Wise Woman'); 'For tooten snooten!' ('Grandmother's Basket'); and 'doozy' ('Old Mother Holle'). They are all nonsensical phrases that my own children used when they were very young.

I have chosen to give a phonetic spelling for two foreign phrases to make the pronunciation easier for young readers. 'Bow sha moy!' ('Grandmother's Basket') is a phonetically spelled Russian exclamation, meaning 'Oh my God!', and 'La Bruha' ('The Beautiful Crone of Córdoba') is a phonetic rendition of the Spanish 'La Bruja', meaning 'witch'.

THE MIDWIFE AND THE DJINN
Leslau, Charlotte and Wolf (ed.), *African Folk Tales,* The Peter Pauper Press, New York, 1963.

THE OLD WOMAN WHO WAS NOT AFRAID
Hearn, Lafcadio, *Japanese Fairy Tales,* The Peter Pauper Press, New York, 1948.

GRANDMOTHER'S BASKET
Barchers, Suzanne I., *Wise Women, Folk and Fairy Tales from Around the World,* Libraries Unlimited, Englewood, Colorado, 1990.

THE WOMAN IN THE MOON
Colum, Padraic, *At the Gateways of the Day,* Oxford University Press, London, 1924.

THE BEAUTIFUL CRONE OF CÓRDOBA
Janvier, Thomas (ed.), *Legends of the City of Mexico,* Harper and Brothers, New York and London, 1910.

GO ASK THE WISE WOMAN
Carter, Angela (ed.), *The Old Wives' Fairy Tale Book,* Pantheon Books, New York, 1990.
Danaher, Kevin, *Folktales of the Irish Countryside,* Mercier Press, Cork, 1967.

OLD MOTHER HOLLE
Budapest, Zsuzsanna E., *Grandmothers of the Moon,* HarperSanFrancisco, 1991.
Gimbutas, Marija, *The Language of the Goddess* and *The Civilization of the Goddess,* HarperSanFrancisco, 1989 and 1991.

THE OLD WOMAN WHO WAS RIGHT
Booss, Claire (ed.), *Scandanavian Folk and Fairy Tales,* Avenel Books, New York, 1984.
Carter, Angela (ed.), *The Old Wives' Fairy Tale Book,* Pantheon Books, New York, 1990.
Yolen, Jane, *Favorite Folktales from Around the World,* Pantheon Books, New York, 1986.